Proverbs 22:6 "Train a child in the way he should go

I Like
To Pray
When...

Practical prayers for a child's everyday life.

By Kim Carlone

Illustrated By: Frank Balesteri and Brianna Carlone

I dedicate this book to my best friend, Jesus.

THANK YOU! THANK YOU! THANK YOU! THANK YOU!

I would like to extend my gratitude to
Mr. Mike Snyder for all of his help with this project and
to his 2010 Web Design students at
Kennard-Dale High School in Fawn Grove, Pennsylvania.

THANK YOU! THANK YOU! THANK YOU! THANK YOU!

A special note from the Author:

In the aftermath of the tragic Sandy Hook Elementary School shooting, I was deeply moved, as I am sure everyone was. So many innocent children lost their lives. I cried out, "Jesus, I don't understand. I pray every day for protection over our schools, over our innocent, helpless children. Now I feel so helpless. What can I do?" To which he simply replied, "Teach them to call on My name."

I had written this book over eight years ago and tried to publish it, to no avail. However, I believe the timing wasn't right. I believe the time is now. I'm sure all parents feel as I do. They want their children protected and are in constant fear with all the tragedies that seem to happen more frequently. I also believe whether you are a parent or not, news of a child's tragic death hits you harder than that of an adult losing a life.

Now that God has been taken out of our public schools, we need Him more than ever. I pray that you will put this book in the hands of each and every child that you come in contact with, whether you are their parent, relative, or friend. Whether the child is a Christian or doesn't know Jesus at all, there is a section in the book that invites him or her to receive Jesus.

Parents, please engage in this book with your child, creating different scenarios in which the child can call on Jesus.

The time is now to stand up and take action. Let us save our innocent, helpless children.

In Jesus' Name,

Kim Carlone

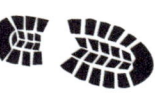

Hi My name is Anthony and I like to pray. The reason God created us a long time ago was to have a relationship with Him. He then gave us His son, Jesus, who died for us on the cross. God wants us to pray and form a close relationship with His son, Jesus. Why do I like to pray? It helps me, especially when I am sad, angry and afraid. It's also a way of talking to Jesus and spending time with Him. It's so easy. I can do it anytime and anywhere because I can do it without speaking out loud; I just speak it in my head. My mom taught me how to pray when I first started talking, I think. She always tells me that we need to pray and spend time with Jesus to live the life that He wants us to have.

I have learned that when I have a problem, all I have to do is call on Jesus and look to the Bible for the right thing to do. The only way to talk to God is through Jesus. The Bible is God's word that He uses to teach us His ways, and His way is always the right way.

If you already know about Jesus, then this book can help you develop a closer relationship with Him.

If you've never been told about Jesus, that's okay, too. At the end of this book you can invite Him into your life.

So let's get started, and I'll share with you when I like to pray…

I like to pray when I'm at the bus stop or riding to school.

Anthony's Problem:

Sometimes I get a little nervous before school, wondering what kind of day I'm going to have. That's why I have a special prayer that I pray.

Dear Jesus,

Please let me have a great day today. Let me be kind to all of the children, even if they're not kind to me. Please protect me, my school and our school's buses.

Scripture Verse: Psalm 121:2

My help comes from the Lord, the maker of heaven and earth.

I like to pray when I feel angry.

Anthony's Problem:

At school, I was walking up to the front of the class when someone tripped me. I was so mad! I wanted to find out who did it and yell at him. Then I remembered my special prayer and walked back to my desk and prayed.

Dear Jesus,

Please help me to get along with everyone and be kind to all of the children, even if they are not kind to me.

Scripture Verse: 1 John 4:11

Dear friends, since God so loved us, we also ought to love one another.

I like to pray when I feel distracted.

Anthony's Problem:

Mr. Huxtable was explaining our homework assignment. My friend wanted to tell me about the video game she was bringing over to my house after school. I really wanted to hear about it, but then I remembered my special prayer and prayed.

Dear Jesus,

Please help me to listen and learn from my teacher right now. Even though I want to talk to my friend, I know that I will be able to later at recess.

Scripture Verse: Proverbs 1:5

Let the wise listen and add to their learning.

I like to pray when I feel unwanted.

<u>Anthony's Problem:</u>

I was waiting as the Kickball Captains picked their teams. I felt so sad because I was the last one to get picked. Why didn't anyone want to choose me? Then I remembered my special prayer and prayed.

Dear Jesus,

Please help me to cheer up and play my best for my team. I know that you have chosen me to be your child and that you have a special plan for me.

Scripture Verse: Isaiah 41:9

I have chosen you and have not rejected you.

I like to pray when I feel hurt.

<u>Anthony's Problem:</u>

Today, we were having races in gym. While I was running, I heard one of the kids call me a name because I wasn't running that fast. I was so upset, I wanted to call him a name back. Then I remembered my special prayer and prayed.

Dear Jesus,

Please help me to forgive the kids when they are mean and call me names. I know that calling them a name back will just make everything worse.

Scripture Verse: 1 Peter 3:9

Do not repay evil with evil or insult with insult.

I like to pray when I feel like lying.

<u>Anthony's Problem:</u>

I was chewing gum in class. The teacher looked over and asked me if I had gum in my mouth. I wanted to lie so I wouldn't get into trouble. Then I remembered my special prayer and prayed.

Dear Jesus,

Please help me to accept my punishment and tell the truth. I know that telling a lie just makes everything worse.

Scripture Verse: Proverbs 12:22

The Lord detests lying lips, but he delights in men who are truthful.

I like to pray when I feel selfish.

Anthony's Problem:

We were outside playing baseball in my backyard. It was my turn to bat. Just then my mom called me in to do my homework. I didn't want to go inside; I wanted to keep playing. Then, I remembered my special prayer and prayed.

Dear Jesus,

Please help me to do my homework with a good attitude. I would rather be playing outside with my friends, but I know that I must obey my parents.

Scripture Verse: Colossians 3:20

Children, obey your parents in everything, for this pleases the Lord.

I like to pray when I feel thankful.

<u>Anthony's Problem:</u>

After I complained about what was for dinner, I learned that some people do not even have enough food to eat. It made me feel thankful and sad at the same time. Then I remembered my special prayer and prayed.

Dear Jesus,

Please help all those who need food. God is great. God is good. Now we thank him for our food. By His hands we all are fed. Thank you, Lord, for our daily bread.

Scripture Verse: Jeremiah 33:11

Give thanks to the Lord Almighty, for the Lord is good.

I like to pray when I feel proud.

Anthony's Problem:

I was telling my parents all about my day and the good decisions that I made. I suddenly remembered that I didn't thank Jesus for all of His help today. Then I remembered my special prayer and prayed.

Dear Jesus,

Thank you for spending the day with me. Thank you for listening and answering all of my prayers today.

 Scripture Verse: John 16:23

I tell you the truth, my Father will give you whatever you ask in my name.

I like to pray when I feel afraid.

<u>Anthony's Problem:</u>

As I was trying to fall asleep, I heard noises outside my window. I was scared and couldn't fall asleep. Then I remembered my special prayer and prayed.

Dear Jesus,

I know that if I am ever afraid, all I have to do is call your name, Jesus. Please protect me and my family and watch over us all through the night.

Scripture Verse: Psalm 4:8

I will lie down and sleep in peace, for you alone, O Lord, make me dwell in safety.

So, what did you think? Easy, isn't it? No matter what your problem is, Jesus is waiting to help you. I feel like He is my best friend.

If you don't know Jesus and would like to invite Him into your life, all you have to do is ask Him through prayer. He wants to be your Savior and your best friend, too. Here is a good way to ask Him:

Dear Jesus,

I know that I have sinned, because I have done and said wrong things. I do not want to be apart from God because of my sin. I need you to take away my sin and forgive me. I believe that God sent you to the Earth for us. You died and rose from the grave for me so my sins could be forgiven because you love me so much. Thank you, Jesus, for forgiving my sins and coming into my life. Please help me to know you more every day. Help me to live the life you want me to live.

Amen.

CONGRATULATIONS!

You are now a child of God! God has made you brand new through His son, and He has great things planned for you.

GREAT NEWS!

I have more great news for you! God's Holy Spirit now lives inside of you and will be with you wherever you go, no matter what you do, for the rest of your life.

Children, always remember: If you are scared or need help, pray to Jesus. He will always help you.

Jesus Laughing

Jesus and _____ best friends.

ABOUT THE AUTHOR

A Christian Mother with a passion for helping children become the person that God created them to be.

Kim currently resides in her home town of Portsmouth, RI with her family.

CPSIA information can be obtained at www.ICGtesting.com
Printed in the USA
BVOW10s1107140814

362888BV00003B/5/P